Harmonies of the Hidden Glade

In the glade where shadows play,
Squirrels sing and dance all day.
A raccoon for a DJ spins,
While rabbits join with silly grins.

A turtle with a top hat bows,
Telling jokes to frolicking cows.
The trees sway with laughter clear,
As nature's band plays without fear.

Original title:
Grove of Grace

Copyright © 2025 Creative Arts Management OÜ
All rights reserved.

Author: Milo Harrington
ISBN HARDBACK: 978-1-80567-023-0
ISBN PAPERBACK: 978-1-80567-103-9

Serenity in the Shade

Underneath a leafy dome,
Bumblebees make honeycomb.
A lazy cat naps on a stump,
While ants prepare a little jump.

They practice dance with tiny feet,
Creating moves both smooth and sweet.
The shadows giggle, light as air,
As critters frolic everywhere.

Timeless Roots of Tranquility

Roots entwined, they plot and plan,
To prank the passing woodland man.
With acorns aimed like mini bombs,
They giggle while the breeze calm.

A wise old owl hoots with glee,
As his friends hide behind a tree.
With feathers fluffed, they take their chance,
To launch a wild surprise dance.

Dreams Weaving through the Foliage

Through the leaves, dreams twist and weave,
Like threads of fun, there's much to believe.
A fox wearing shades struts by,
While butterflies simply sigh.

They play hopscotch on the sunbeams,
Creating laughter, sparking dreams.
With every twist, or every turn,
In this realm, the joy will burn.

Enchanted Fragments of Nature's Heart

In a patch where the squirrels play,
The trees sport hats made of hay.
A bunny races past with flair,
While whispers travel in the air.

A lizard sunbathes on a log,
Wearing sunglasses, what a smog!
The flowers giggle in the breeze,
Tickled by the buzzing bees.

A fairy lost her shoe today,
Claiming fruit flies led her astray.
A pixie joined in just for fun,
Together they danced under the sun.

As twilight wraps the scene in gold,
Magic stories start to unfold.
With chuckles echoing through the night,
Nature's heart beats pure delight.

Epiphanies Among the Ferns

In the ferns where secrets creep,
A hedgehog's snoring sounds quite deep.
Two frogs debate on who is the best,
Their croaking tune, a puzzling jest.

A wise old owl wears a crown,
He's the king of this woodland town.
His subjects plot their silly shows,
With juggling acorns, anything goes.

A cricket taps a funky beat,
While ants form lines to take a seat.
They laugh at jokes of wiggly worms,
And share their dreams of chestnut perms.

Underneath the playful skies,
Nature winks with twinkling eyes.
Each leaf a laugh, each branch a cheer,
In this leafy world, joy is near.

Carved Stories on Bark and Branch

On the trunks where characters hide,
Raccoons plot their next nighttime ride.
Between the grooves, tales come alive,
As squirrels rehearse their comedy jive.

Woodpeckers drum a quirky beat,
Tick-tock, they dance on their tiny feet.
A shy deer blushes at their show,
As butterflies giggle in the glow.

A chubby chipmunk steals the scene,
Wearing a hat of shiny green.
He proclaims himself a fashion king,
While birds all chirp and merrily sing.

As stars peek through the leafy dome,
Nature spins tales that feel like home.
With every bark and every branch,
A world of laughter takes a chance.

A Symphony in the Sylvan Silence

In the hush where giggles collide,
You'll find the fox with nothing to hide.
He juggles rocks while hopping high,
Making the clouds above just sigh.

Fairies holding a talent show,
With twinkling lights and a sparkly glow.
A snail performs the slowest dance,
While laughter flares and dreams entrance.

The wind hums tunes that twirl and twist,
As nature's performers can't be missed.
Each rustle brings a tease or slap,
A playful game perhaps, a trap?

So gather near this woodland stage,
Where joy and folly take the page.
In every leaf and shout that flies,
A symphony of giggles lies.

The Language of Leaves in the Breeze

Whispers of leaves in a giggly dance,
A breeze tells jokes, if you give it a chance.
Branches shake hands, they bump and tease,
Frolicking softly with the sassy trees.

Squirrels crack jokes with nuts in their paws,
Tickling the branches with playful applause.
A leaf falls down just to steal the show,
Landing on a critter, 'Hey, don't you know?'

Every gust carries chuckles to share,
As shadows stretch long, they float in the air.
Laughter erupts from the roots to the tips,
Nature's own comedy, complete with quips.

In this lively stage under skies so wide,
Every twig is a friend, the trees take pride.
Listen real close, you'll hear nature's cheer,
In this funny world, joy is always near.

The Sanctuary of Twilight Glades

In twilight's embrace, the fireflies spark,
Lighting comedy acts in the stillening dark.
Beneath bending boughs in a jester's court,
Moonbeams join in for the laughter they'll sport.

An owl hoots puns with a serious face,
While rabbits breakdance in a leafy place.
Beneath the big stars, they plan their big show,
With props made of acorns, oh, what a glow!

Funny fragments of night flutter around,
Crickets are the chorus making sweet sound.
As everything chuckles, the grass joins, too,
In this whimsical space, where dreams come true.

With giggles and whispers, the night rolls its eyes,
As shadows join in for a dance in disguise.
Laughter embraces all creatures that roam,
In twilight's soft arms, every heart finds home.

Lullabies Beneath the Canopy

When night softly falls, the leaves hum along,
While critters croon gently to nature's sweet song.
The moon plays a tune on its silvery strings,
Bringing giggles and grins to all of the beings.

Little ones snuggle in mossy retreats,
While fireflies flicker in their fuzzy seats.
"Why did the acorn grow a mustache?" they tease,
"Such style for a nut - oh, if only a breeze!"

The lullabies whisper through twirls and spins,
As branches play tag where the fun never ends.
Each note is a tickle, a hug from the night,
Even the owls can't help but take flight!

Under the dark, where dreams can collide,
Napping and laughing, the world feels like pride.
With chuckles on leaves, the night dances free,
A bedtime of joy, where all are carefree.

Threads of Gold in the Green

Amidst greenery woven with gold's gentle hue,
There's mischief afoot, as the critters all do.
A squirrel in a hat, looking dapper and spry,
Waves at the butterfly fluttering by.

The daisies play cards, while the daisies plead,
"Play fair, little grass, you're not yet a seed!"
A snake coils up, sharing stories of jest,
While the sun peeks out, giving flowers a rest.

With giggles of petals, the color runs wild,
As daisies are rumbling, and the wind is a child.
Twirling in circles, they spin to the tune,
In a wacky old dance under the light of the moon.

So come, take a stroll through this lively ole place,
Where nature's a comedian, leading the chase.
With threads bright and golden in a quilt of pure glee,
Let's laugh with the leaves, as silly as can be!

The Solace of Sylvan Whispers

The trees gossip all day long,
With tales of birds that sing off-key.
Squirrels debate who has the best nuts,
While mockingbirds steal their TV.

Fallen leaves play hide and seek,
With acorns that roll with glee,
A wise old owl cracks silly jokes,
While beetles dance, as happy as can be.

Branches sway like they're hip-hop stars,
With chipmunks joining in the beat.
But watch your step, oh clumsy foot,
For roots are sneaky at your feet!

In this silly sylvan scene,
Each rustle brings a laugh, not dread.
Nature's playground filled with joy,
Where giggles dwell and stress has fled.

Nectar of Nature's Embrace

Bumblebees wear tiny hard hats,
As flowers flaunt their vibrant hues.
Insects hold a grand ballet,
While sunbeams cheer from leafy views.

The buzzing choir sings off-key,
While ladybugs strut with flair.
A parade of ants in a conga line,
Who knew they'd take such care?

Mirth in the petals, laughter in air,
The daisy winks with cheeky style.
"Pollinate this!" calls out the breeze,
Helping all the blooms compile.

Sweet nectar flows like gossip, quick,
With every sip a chuckle blooms.
Join the party, nature's fun,
In this wild, whimsical room!

The Treetops' Silent Symphony

High above, the branches twirl,
Conducting breezes with a shove.
The leaves rustle, sharing secrets,
While clouds float by and laugh in love.

A squirrel on a summit, bold,
Balances nuts atop his crown.
The winds chuckle at his stunts,
It's nature's show, don't wear a frown.

Crows caw like they're comedians,
Cracking jokes 'bout far-off cays.
"Oh, the trouble that we've seen!"
They jest, while sunbeams do ballet.

In the stillness of this concert,
A symphony of funny sights.
Where everything's a bit absurd,
And joy springs forth in all delights.

A Canopy of Calm and Clarity

Under the leafy overhead,
Lies a throne of twigs and dreams.
Grass tickles toes while ants parade,
In this realm of giggles and schemes.

A lizard lounges, sunglasses on,
While crickets try their karaoke.
"Sing louder!" chirps a wise old tree,
And the sun shines down, so carefree.

Mushrooms giggle at the creeping snails,
Who can't keep pace, but don't lose fun.
A dance-off breaks between the roots,
Under the watch of the cheerful sun.

Relax, refresh, let laughter reign,
In this sanctuary of light.
Where nature bends to pure delight,
And everything just feels so right.

A Celebration of Silent Moments

In the stillness where we stand,
Even the squirrels have a plan.
They plot and scheme with tiny hands,
As we all laugh, oh isn't it grand?

A butterfly lands on my nose,
I sneeze, and then it promptly goes.
The echoes of our giggles rise,
While petals drift with joyful sighs.

A rabbit hops to join the fun,
Wearing sunglasses, oh what a run!
We dance in circles, laughter loud,
Underneath the sky, so proud.

The trees are swaying side to side,
With gnarly limbs, they seem to hide.
They whisper secrets, tiptoe near,
As we toast to nonsense and good cheer.

Nature's Palette of Healing Hues

In gardens bright, a painter's dream,
With purple blooms and golden gleam.
Though bees are buzzing all around,
They mind their business, none are browned.

The daisies giggle in the wind,
While roses blush as if they've sinned.
A yellow frog begins to croak,
And joins our laughter with a joke.

A dandelion in full show,
Winks at us, as if to know,
That all our worries drift away,
On fluffy clouds of bright display.

We splash through puddles, muddy mess,
In nature's art, we find success.
With every hue, a silly smile,
Each step we take is worth the while.

The Hush of Forgotten Paths

A winding trail tells tales so sweet,
With every turn, a silly feat.
I trip on roots, but what a grace,
As leaves above hide a laughing face.

A whispering breeze swirls all around,
While squirrels giggle, oh, what a sound!
They point at me with little paws,
As I pretend to take a pause.

An owl looks down with squinty eyes,
I wink back, to my surprise.
Its feathered brow raises in glee,
As if it knows all my blunders, wee.

We stroll the paths, side by side,
Where secrets and laughter can't abide.
These forgotten ways, where joy's amassed,
One silly step, and I'm outclassed.

Soft Murmurs Among the Pines

Among the pines, we share our jest,
Where squirrels put silence to the test.
They tiptoe on branches, oh what a sight,
As we slip and chuckle into the night.

The fragrance of spruce fills the air,
While humorous shadows dance with flair.
A raccoon peeks from behind a tree,
As if to join our band of glee.

The whispers of nature, soft and sly,
Seem to conspire, oh my, oh my!
Every rustle feels like a prank,
As I trip over roots and fall in a tank.

With giggles and snorts, we roam this place,
Finding joy in every untamed space.
In this wild wood, where we just should,
Unleash our laughter, as only we could.

Chasing Shadows in Sunlit Play

In a dance of light and shade,
Little feet do prance and fade,
Amidst the trees, they twist and twirl,
Laughing at the leaves that swirl.

An old owl watches with a wink,
While squirrels plot and pause to think,
Where did that shadow bounce and roll?
Oh, the joy of a playful stroll!

Beneath the branches, giggles soar,
As sunlight spills on forest floor,
A game of hide and seek unfolds,
With whispers and tales yet untold.

But watch your step, oh little mate,
For toads might leap and curse your fate,
As you chase those shadows deep and wide,
In the sunlit tales where mischief hides.

The Enigma of the Elm and Ash

Two trees stand tall, with secrets vast,
The age-old battle of shadows cast,
One says, "I'm taller, can't you see?"
The other retorts, "Just wait for me!"

Leaves gossip about the comical feud,
As critters munch and grunt, quite rude,
'Twixt branches, wise tales of who is best,
While owls chuckle, all too blessed.

At night, the stars lend a bemused ear,
As branches whisper, "No need to fear!"
A riddle unwrapped with every breeze,
In the playful banter of the trees.

So next you stroll where boughs intertwine,
Imagine these trees sipping fine wine,
Debating the silliest of things,
A raucous laugh that nature brings.

Ciphers in the Heart of the Forest

What's hidden where the wild things hide?
A puzzle wrapped in nature's pride,
With mossy stones that wink and tease,
And vines that giggle in the breeze.

A hedgehog scribbles codes of wonder,
As birds exchange a tune of thunder,
The trees hum softly in discord,
While bees bumble about their board.

Deciphering laughter in the air,
There's a riddle with each twig laid bare,
Nature's script, a funny mix,
With beech and birch painting their tricks.

So gather 'round and let's rejoice,
In these whispers that make us voice,
The ciphers carved in leaf and bark,
Where every secret leaves a mark.

The Art of Stillness in Green Light

Amidst the calm of green delight,
Invisible jokes take off in flight,
While nature holds its quiet show,
The art of stillness beginning to glow.

A snail recites an epic tale,
While slugs don armor, slick and pale,
In motionless grace, the whispers thread,
Of laughter shared through leaves instead.

The breeze, a silent chuckler too,
Brushes by with a soft, clever woo,
As shadows yawn beneath the sun,
Proclaiming peace and silly fun.

So find your pause in this green glow,
A merry stillness, just take it slow,
For in the quiet, laughter waits,
In nature's arms, where joy creates.

Time in the Thicket of Tranquility.

In the thicket, squirrels plot,
Nutty schemes and acorn thoughts,
Birds are giggling, what a sight,
Chasing shadows, taking flight.

Rabbits hop with twinkling eyes,
Making popcorn from the pies,
Sneaky foxes in disguise,
Cracking jokes beneath blue skies.

Trees sway gently, dancing leaf,
While the ants are thieves, oh grief,
Stealing crumbs left by the feast,
Planning parties, to say the least.

Frogs in pools with tiny crowns,
Making ribbits, wearing frowns,
Lost their way on lily pads,
What a day, it's all so mad!

Whispers in the Canopy

Leaves are rustling, whispers flow,
As the wind joins in the show,
Witty whispers high above,
Chirping secrets of the dove.

Butterflies wear tiny hats,
Doing dance with prancing cats,
A playful breeze gives them a spin,
Around and around, let's begin!

Mice are plotting great escapes,
In their dream of cake-shaped grapes,
With tiny maps and goofy grins,
Planning parties where fun begins.

Squirrels hold a nutty court,
Debating snacks as their sport,
Underneath a canopy bright,
Laughter echoes, pure delight.

Beneath the Boughs of Serenity

Beneath the branches, shadows play,
Funny antics make their way,
Beetles march with tiny drums,
While the hedgehogs hum, here comes!

Chairs of leaves, they all recline,
Telling tales of wild design,
A parrot's joke, a turtle's tune,
Laughter wrapped in bright cocoon.

Frogs with shades sip lemonade,
While the grasshoppers parade,
Bugs compose a comedy,
Nature's jest in symphony.

Bunnies play a game of chase,
With clumsy steps, they set the pace,
All around the soft green space,
Laughter dances at their grace.

Echoes of a Gentle Dawn

Morning breaks with snickers bright,
Sunshine tickles, what a sight,
In the grass, a sleepy cat,
Yarns a tale of things that sat.

A rooster crows with silly flair,
Bouncing up and down, beware,
While a horse rolls in the dew,
Making muffins, oh, he knew!

Clouds drift by with silly hats,
While the foxes joke with bats,
Every critter has a part,
In the morning's silly art.

As the day begins to wake,
Nature laughs, and no one fakes,
In this space where fun is found,
Joy reverberates all around.

Lanterns of Light in Leafy Halls

In the canopy, shadows play,
Laughter echoes, come what may.
Squirrels dance in acorn hats,
While birds debate on silly chats.

Mossy seats for ants on break,
Telling tales of the pie they bake.
Under leaves, a quirky light,
Flickers like a firefly's flight.

Conversations with the Elder Trees

Old oaks gossip about the wind,
Share wild stories they rescind.
Maples blush with green delight,
While birches chirp, 'Watch your height!'

Roots stretch out to catch a pun,
As willow winks, 'This is fun!'
Creeks chuckle with a gentle flow,
Nature laughs, and so we go.

Flickers of Gold in the Twilight Whisper

Golden glimmers, fireflies in tow,
Whisper secrets only they know.
Crickets tune their nighttime song,
While frogs join in, playing along.

The moon peeks through with a cheeky grin,
A raccoon smiles, 'Let the fun begin!'
With each flicker, joy takes flight,
In the hush of the fading light.

The Stillness of the Between

In the quiet, mice hold debates,
Discussing cheese and garden gates.
A lazy cat naps on a log,
Dreaming of chasing a friendly frog.

Sunbeams ticking like a clock,
The world slows, just to talk.
Deep in nature, laughter steeps,
As even the flowers take their peeps.

Unraveling Threads of Nature's Tale

In a garden where giggles grow,
A gopher wore a bow and toe.
He danced around with quite a flair,
While worms took notes, in disbelief, staring.

The daisies chuckled, swayed on trails,
As squirrels debated their cheese-filled tales.
Crickets chirped, trying twirls at night,
While a snail won gold for the slowest flight.

Butterflies stashed away their pride,
With lavish wings, they tried to glide.
They crashed in bushes, a comic mess,
As ladybugs cheered their leafy dress.

Nature spun jokes, like webs in air,
Bees buzzed laughter with every flare.
Through all the chaos, joy took root,
In threads of the wild, nature found its scoot.

Harmony Found Where Hearts Align

Two owls hooted their funny tune,
Beneath the light of the chubby moon.
A raccoon joined in, wearing a hat,
As frogs croaked rhythms, tipping their mat.

Bunnies bounced, forgetting their care,
In a circle dance without a scare.
Chasing their tails, they twirled with glee,
While hedgehogs chuckled, set their cups free.

The owls held a talent show at dawn,
And the skunks performed, but nobody yawned.
With laughter soaring on gentle breeze,
They found sweet harmony among the trees.

In every heart, a beat did thrum,
Nature giggled as creatures hum.
For in this patch, so wild and true,
Aligning hearts brought laughter anew.

The Spirit Song of the Seasons

Spring sang sweetly, but tripped in cheer,
With flowers sneezing, oh my, oh dear!
While summer danced in a flip-flop race,
The sunbeams laughed as they tried to chase.

Autumn strolled with a leaf parade,
But a gust came by, their plans delayed.
Pumpkins rolled, giggling past the pines,
While squirrels wore acorns for hats and signs.

Winter wobbled on ice with glee,
But fell in a snowdrift, a sight to see!
Frosty chuckled, but glimmered bright,
As snowflakes danced like stars at night.

Throughout the year, their jests will flow,
Nature's spirit puts on quite the show.
With every change, they laugh and play,
A song of seasons, that's here to stay.

A Healing Journey in Hidden Places

In a nook where the ferns take a break,
A turtle whispered, "For goodness' sake!"
The hedgehogs giggled and bounced with glee,
As they found the light underneath the tree.

A secret path with laughter bounds,
Where the flowers speak in sweet, silly sounds.
Chasing butterflies, a merry race,
As raccoons joined in to find their place.

Hidden spots with sunlight streams,
A patch of dreams and silly themes.
With every turn, a chuckle brings,
A healing dance beneath nature's wings.

In laughter's charm, the heart expands,
Exploring the world, with little hands.
Through twists and turns, we find such grace,
In hidden places, we find our space.

A Sanctuary Beneath the Sky

Under starlit dreams we prance,
Dancing shadows, in a trance.
Squirrels plotting mischief proud,
Whisper secrets, laugh aloud.

In the night the owls declare,
What's that smell? Is it bear hair?
With acorns flying, watch your head,
Nature's humor, laughter spread.

Branches wave, like arms at play,
As if to say, 'Join us today!'
A wild party, vines entwine,
Where the ridiculous meets divine.

With each wind, a giggle flows,
Tickling toes from head to toes.
In this haven, puns take flight,
Under stars of pure delight.

The Breath of Ancient Trees

Those trees are old, and so they claim,
They've seen it all, but bring the shame.
With wrinkled bark and hollow eyes,
They mock the youth with their wise cries.

Rabbits hopping in the race,
Chasing dreams in a leafy space.
Whispers of age, yet lively still,
Shaking leaves with a hearty thrill.

The crickets sing out silly songs,
While the fox trots by, it hardly throngs.
Nature's jesters, all in tune,
Beneath the light of the winking moon.

A tree stump throne, where I recline,
With every bark, I sip my wine.
In this place where laughter grows,
Even roots have punchlines that flows.

Moonlit Reveries in the Thicket

Amidst the shrubs, the moonlight glows,
With every rustle, laughter flows.
The nightingale bird sings a joke,
While nearby, a bushy tailed bloke.

Fireflies twinkle, a dance so bright,
With giggles that chase away the night.
A raccoon with snacks, can't hide his grin,
Rummaging through all that's been pinned.

Beneath the stars, we spin and sway,
Chasing shadows that frolic and play.
Each sound a tune, each laugh a rhyme,
As nature throws its punchlines in time.

In this thicket where dreams collide,
The laughter bonds, a joyful tide.
So let the moon, our witness be,
To the merry chaos under the tree.

Sanctuary of Stillness and Solitude

In the calm, where silence reigns,
Echoes of chuckles ooze through the veins.
A turtle slinks with swagger proud,
While chips of laughter form a cloud.

The stillness steals the show tonight,
Yet whispers bubble, full of delight.
A breeze that tickles, a whispering tease,
With every creak, it's nature's glees.

Here we find a merry nook,
With a soothing laugh, come take a look.
A world so quiet, yet bold and vast,
Where moments linger, and giggles last.

In solitude, a jest we share,
A peaceful space, beyond compare.
With nature's arms, we hold our laughs,
In a sanctuary of playful paths.

Beneath the Boughs of Serenity

There's a tree with a hat made of leaves,
Birds gossip on branches, sharing their heaves.
Squirrels debate on who's got the best nut,
As they dance and prance, oh, what a big rut!

A raccoon rolls dice; is he counting the stars?
While the owls wonder who's tuning their guitars.
The breeze steals a joke, but it giggles too fast,
And a bunny just snorts, 'Man, this day's a blast!'

Among odd-shaped trunks, laughter echoes out,
Mushrooms sway gently, while the frogs scream and shout.
A snail's slow waltz makes everyone cheer,
"Hey, slowpoke!" they shout, "Have you been drinking beer?"

In this place where the wild creatures play,
Giggles and rumbles make for a great day.
Beneath leafy layers, life's a grand mess,
Each chuckle's a treasure, can't help but confess!

Lullabies of Leaf and Lichen

In the nighttime's quilt, the fireflies glow,
While mice tap their tap shoes, putting on a show.
Frogs croon sweet nothings, romantic and bold,
And a hedgehog rolls over, his stories retold.

Leaves sway like dancers, twirling on air,
While a wise old owl spins, but he doesn't care.
The moon grins above, amused by the sight,
As a snail sings a ballad, trying to take flight.

Moss cushions the laughter of critters nearby,
As the crickets compose, with a sigh and a why.
"Why do we dance?" the young firefly beams,
"Because in a world like this, we live in dreams!"

So under the stars, with a chuckle and cheer,
They laugh at the shadows that wiggle and leer.
In this whimsical realm, where odd things align,
Nature hums sweet lullabies while sipping on wine.

Secrets Held in Twisted Roots

In the tangled embrace of roots down below,
A tiny ant cackles at all of the show.
She whispers of secrets and nonsense, oh dear,
While a beetle throws tantrums, full of hot air!

Fungi hold meetings, discussing their plans,
While a snake slithers by, dreaming of jams.
"I'm a disco!" he hisses, and shines in the dark,
As the worms break it down with a wiggle and spark.

Twisted and tangled, the stories unfold,
Of how every critter's been brave and bold.
A commotion erupts when a butterfly slips,
And a hedgehog stands tall, sharing his quips.

From below the ground, to branches above,
Each creature reveals a funny little shove.
In the crooked old roots, where the tales intertwine,
There's laughter to be found, perfect, pure, divine!

The Embrace of Verdant Dreams

In the arms of the green, silliness thrives,
Where the daisies tell tales, of their outlandish lives.
A caterpillar grins, "I'm still working on me,
But wait till you see what I'm destined to be!"

With a wink and a sway, the daisies confide,
"Let's dance in the dirt, and let giggles collide!"
A bumblebee buzzes, "Hey, what's in a name?
I'm a honey connoisseur, and I'm here for the fame!"

As the sunset drips gold, laughter rings out,
Raccoons play peekaboo, oh, what's it about?
"Hey, rabbit, don't hop away, join in the hype,
We're about to create the world's first bug type!"

Thus beneath the canopy, with dreams that entice,
Nature spins tales, all sugary and nice.
In this friendly cocoon, we all laugh and beam,
For in the embrace of one another, we dream!

Shadows of Solitude and Solace

In quiet corners, shadows dance,
They prance and twirl, take a chance.
A squirrel debates on a grander plan,
While pondering life, with a nut in hand.

A breeze tickles the leaves so lightly,
They giggle and sway, oh so sprightly.
A raccoon pauses, mid-moonlit plot,
His bandit mask says he's up to a lot.

A wise old owl, with spectacles round,
Reads tales of mischief, the wildest found.
With every hoot, he shares a grin,
Spinning tales where hilarity begins.

Under the stars, mischief abounds,
From clumsy deer to the rustle ofounds.
In shadows cast by the moon's soft glow,
Solitude laughs, in whispers low.

Trails of Light in the Wilderness

On trails of light, the sun likes to play,
With wiggly worms who waltz all day.
A bunny in shades, so cool and bright,
Sips herbal tea, 'It's a lovely night!'

Bushes giggle as birds on a line,
Swap silly gossip with grapevine wine.
The trees roll their bark, chuckles unwind,
As sunbeams dance, leaving worries behind.

A fox in a hat, quite debonair,
Holds a dance-off with the fresh country air.
With every hop and silly twist,
Nature's laugh is impossible to resist.

On trails where light and laughter collide,
Wilderness winks, it's a joyful ride.
Every step brings a chuckle anew,
In nature's embrace, find joy to pursue.

The Garden of Whispered Wishes

In a garden where gnomes share tea,
They tickle the daisies, what a sight to see!
With wishes whispered to the breeze,
The flowers giggle, swaying with ease.

A snail with a dream, wearing a cape,
Claims to be fast, 'No need for escape!'
But while he boasts of journeys grand,
A butterfly zooms and takes a stand.

Toads croak sonnets, what a sly crew,
While ladybugs gossip, their voices anew.
Each stem a story, full of delight,
Where whimsy blooms in the soft moonlight.

In this haven where laughter swells,
Whispered wishes weave their spells.
Every chuckle, a promise kept,
In the garden of dreams, where joy is leapt.

Reflections in the Pool of Calm

In a still pool of calm, frogs take their place,
They practice their poses, a splash with grace.
With ripples of laughter, a fish swims by,
A splash-tastic dive! Oh my, oh my!

A turtle in shades gives a slow-motion wink,
'You hurry too much, just stop and think!'
The lily pads giggle, they float in cheer,
As reflections bubble, fun's always near.

The sun waves hello with a golden wink,
While clouds join the party, they pop, they blink.
In this serene theater, silliness reigns,
With every wave, delight entertains.

Reflections bubble, stories they share,
Of whimsical antics and frolicking flair.
In the pool of calm, laughter's the charm,
Where every splash feels like a warm balm.

Whispers of Serene Shadows

In the hush where critters play,
Squirrels dance in a nutty fray.
Robins strut with a cheerful song,
While ants march by, they won't take long.

Beneath the leaf so green and bright,
A frog croaks jokes, what a silly sight!
With every bounce and hop so grand,
He dreams of fame, a band's big stand.

The wind it giggles, sways the trees,
Tickling branches with sweet, soft pleas.
When laughter rings through the calm air,
You'd think the woods had laughter to share.

Under the twinkling glow of stars,
Creatures gather, with snacks in jars.
They enjoy the night, full of jest,
In a woodland party, they feel blessed.

Dance of the Dappled Light

Sunbeams peek through foliage bright,
Playing tag with the leaves in flight.
A bumblebee buzzes a little tune,
Claiming he's the sun's own cartoon.

The shadows jig and wiggle near,
As mockingly they flicker here.
A lizard slips in a chaotic spin,
Claiming top prize for the funniest win.

With laughs that ripple through the glade,
Even the flowers seem unafraid.
Petals chuckle, swaying around,
In this joyful, green, laughing ground.

A puddle tells stories of rain,
Each ripple a giggle, can't contain.
As fireflies dance in the midst of night,
They twinkle like stars, so silly and bright.

Echoes Beneath the Canopy

Beneath the leaves, whispers abound,
As owls share secrets without a sound.
Chipmunks chime in with quirky rhymes,
Counting the acorns, amusing crimes.

The rustling grass plays hide and seek,
While butterflies giggle, so to speak.
A raccoon stumbles, goes tumbling down,
Leaving the forest for a moment of frown.

The branches shake when laughter breaks,
Even the ground lets out some shakes.
Echoes of joy bounce high and low,
In playful banter, the laughter flows.

As night crests in, the stories grow,
With every star, a glimmering glow.
The moonlight chuckles, reflecting the grace,
In this playful, enchanted space.

Harmony in the Heartwood

In the heartwood, where antics thrive,
Woodpeckers knock like they're alive.
A wise old owl croaks puns so grand,
While squirrels giggle, their tails in hand.

The breeze, a joker, brushes by,
Tickling grass, making it sigh.
Crickets chirp a nightly tune,
Under the watching, glimmering moon.

Tree trunks twist in jolly cheer,
Echoing laughter that's crystal clear.
A deer trips over her own sweet feet,
In this woodland ballet, oh so neat!

With every rustle and playful sound,
Joyful spirits dance all around.
It's a woodland caper, light as air,
Where fun and folly find their fair share.

The Tapestry of Green Dreams

In a world where the bushes cheer,
Trees wear hats, oh so dear.
Squirrels dance with a cheeky grin,
As the sun starts to poke its chin.

Beneath the ferns, a rabbit sings,
Of carrot pies and other things.
Leaves whisper secrets, soft and light,
While crickets play in the fading night.

A bushy-tailed thief, so spry,
Steals a blueberry, oh my, oh my!
But when the owl gives a hoot,
The berry's gone—now that's a hoot!

A dappled light paints the ground,
With giggles and laughter all around.
Where every twig might just surprise,
With winking leaves and peek-a-boo skies.

Echoes Beneath the Leafy Arches

Under branches, laughter swells,
Echoing through the leafy bells.
A parrot mimics all our jokes,
While wise old owls just shake and hoax.

Frogs in coats of green and brown,
Hop in rhythm—who wears the crown?
With each splash, the pond will bounce,
As turtles pause to sit and pounce.

Sunlight dapples with a wink,
As dragonflies hover and think.
"Is that a noodle?" one asks with glee,
"Oh no, just a twig," comes the decree.

The air is ripe with giggles bright,
As branches sway with all their might.
In this wild, whimsical scene,
Nature's comedy reigns serene.

Petals and Promises in the Underbrush

Beneath the stems where daisies chat,
A sleepy bee dreams on a mat.
With sticky paws and a giggling hum,
He crashes into soft blooms—oh, what a bum!

Ladybugs toss their polka dots,
While ants march in their funny spots.
A caterpillar steals the show,
With wiggles and jiggles, oh what a glow!

A dandelion wishes to fly,
"Just one puff!" It gives a sigh.
But blown too hard, it spins away,
Now on a cloud, it hopes to stay.

The flowers chuckle in the breeze,
Whispering secrets with such ease.
In every petal, laughter blooms,
As joy erupts from nature's wombs.

Time Slows in the Embrace of Nature

When the clock ticks slow as mud,
And sunshine spills like warm honey flood.
The grass tickles feet in playful delight,
While shadows dance in the fading light.

A bear in shades, all cool and slick,
Hums a tune — it's quite the trick.
With a belly flop, he makes a splash,
While gossiping birds offer a laugh.

Old trees tell tales with knotted glee,
Of how the wind tickled a bumblebee.
Time grins sly as the squirrels pop,
For nature's clock just loves to stop.

Between each leaf, giggles arise,
From sunlit pranks and butterfly flies.
In this slow world, with joy entwined,
Even ticks of time seem so aligned.

Rustle of Leaves in Gentle Murmurs

In a forest where whispers play,
Leaves gossip secrets in a breezy ballet.
Squirrels juggle acorns, oh what a sight!
While birds chirp jokes, taking flight.

Bees buzz, wearing tiny hats,
Dancing around, what chubby fats!
The trees chuckle, swaying with glee,
As mushrooms giggle beneath a wee.

A rabbit hops, with a wiggly nose,
Chasing its shadow, avoiding the blows.
The sun peeks through like a playful cat,
Tickling the grass where the wise toads sat.

Here, laughter echoes among the pines,
A silly romp that intertwines.
With every step, a grin takes place,
In this patch of delight, oh what a race!

A Tapestry Woven in Green

In a patchwork quilt of shades so bright,
Birds wear socks that aren't quite right.
Tree trunks waddle, roots do the jig,
A scene so silly, oh what a gig!

The butterflies wear mismatched shoes,
While chatting with snails in the morning dew.
The flowers wink as they sway in tune,
As bees and crickets throw a wild cartoon.

Frogs join in, looking rather posh,
With tiny top hats in a fanciful wash.
Dancing around in jubilant spins,
Among the blossoms, everyone grins.

Sunset brushes colors in a swirl,
All critters smile in a whimsical whirl.
In this lively patch of nature's glee,
Every leaf and laugh, wild and free!

Refuge Amidst the Flora

Where the wild plants throw a bash,
And trees misplace their branches in a flash.
A hedgehog joins with a glittery bow,
As flowers spin tales we'll never know.

Bunnies in hats serve tea quite grand,
While playing croquet with a cucumber band.
The daisies dance in a whimsical line,
Winking at ladybugs sipping their wine.

A friendly spider knits silly webs,
With dreams of yarn and colorful ebbs.
The ants parade in a march so stout,
Each step a giggle, turning about.

In this refuge of fanciful cheer,
Nature chuckles, bringing us near.
With every rustle in this leafy choir,
Joy and laughter never tire!

Sunbeams and Silhouettes

Sunbeams tumble like clumsy fries,
Lighting up shadows with giggly sighs.
A raccoon juggles its lunch in delight,
While nearby a sunflower takes a bite.

Roaming in circles, the shadows tease,
Swaying like dancers in a summer breeze.
Glimmers of laughter twinkle at dawn,
As crickets compose a tune with a yawn.

The daisies giggle in silly fits,
While ants enjoy stand-up comedy skits.
Every rustle becomes a new pun,
In this merry patch where the sun loves to run.

Evening brings a chorus of chuckles,
With creatures sharing whimsical huddles.
Together they bask in the evening grace,
In a world of humor, a warm embrace!

Shadows of the Ancient Woods

In shadows deep where squirrels dance,
A tree with limbs that seem to prance.
The owls make jokes, they hoot and tease,
While raccoons plot, all aim to please.

A deer with flair, just struts on by,
In snazzy shoes, oh my, oh my!
The mossy floor, a stage so grand,
Where every critter plays its band.

A chipmunk juggles acorns round,
While frogs in tuxedos leap off the ground.
The ancient woods, so full of dreams,
It's where the funny spirit beams.

So join the fun beneath the trees,
Where laughter rustles with the breeze.
And in this land of quirky cheer,
You'll find your smile, loud and clear.

The Music of a Gentle Breeze

The breeze whistles tunes, both soft and sly,
It plays a trick, oh my, oh my!
With leaves that giggle in the sun,
A symphony of nature's fun.

A funny frog conducts the show,
With lilypads, his stage to glow.
While butterflies dance in silly flight,
Marked in hues that delight the sight.

The breeze seems to know all the corny jokes,
As all the trees sway and poke.
The pine trees chuckle, shake their tops,
While elderberries burst out with plops.

So if you wander through this land,
Keep an ear tuned to the fancy band.
For nature sings in a voice so sly,
That makes you laugh, oh so high.

Serenity's Leafy Retreat

In this quiet nook, leaves chatter away,
Where branches gossip, night and day.
The squirrels debate who's got the best stash,
While dandelions laugh, "Oh, what a splash!"

Amidst the ferns, a turtle's slow race,
With that goofy grin on its face.
A breeze that tickles the nose just so,
Sends giggles into the air, don't you know?

A hedgehog rolls, a bundle of cheer,
While crickets strum tunes we all want to hear.
In this leafy retreat, fun takes the lead,
Where every critter knows how to feed.

So come for a visit, don't be aloof,
Join in the laughter, it's the real proof.
In serenity's arms, find joy that's free,
This leafy retreat is a jolly spree.

Reverie under the Ponderosa

Under the Ponderosa's arching spray,
Living life silly, come what may.
With shadows that flicker, the sun plays hide,
As giggles escape from nature's stride.

A porcupine's sport is a prickly hug,
And rabbits engage in a burrow bug.
The pine cones drop, like thoughts gone wild,
Creating laughter, as nature smiled.

A bumblebee buzzes a lively tune,
Flashing its stripes like a lucky rune.
While butterflies do the waltz, oh dear!
Making sure they have fun, never fear!

So lay down your cares, in the piney haze,
Where humor twirls in a playful maze.
In reverie's warmth, you'll find no strife,
Just the funny essence of nature's life.

A Haven for Wandering Souls

In the heart of the woods, the squirrels conspire,
Chasing their dreams on a tightrope of wire.
The owls wear glasses, quite fashionable too,
While frogs critique style in tweed coats of blue.

The moon plays tricks, like a mischievous sprite,
Casting shadows that dance in the soft, silver light.
But watch out for branches that swing like a fist,
They'll whack you on the head, oh, what a twist!

Raccoons discuss politics under the trees,
Gossiping loudly over cups of sweet tea.
The paths are all slippery, thanks to the dew,
And if you trip on a root, they'll all laugh at you!

So come take a stroll where the laughter is found,
In this quirky safe haven, where joy knows no bound.
With each step you take, let your worries all cease,
In this woodland retreat, you'll discover your peace.

Tides of Thunder Among the Trees

The wind whistles tunes like a playful sprite,
As branches do salsa in sheer delight.
Deer try to tango, but stumble in pairs,
While rabbits hold dance-offs without any cares.

Mushrooms spin tales of the storms they have braved,
While the beetles roll dice, feeling quite raved.
And the trees whisper secrets from ages ago,
Of acorns that learned how to put on a show.

The clouds play dodgeball, all fluffy and grand,
As squirrels form teams to take a bold stand.
While the acorns rain down like sprightly confetti,
You'll find yourself laughing, but oh, be ready!

So whenever you stroll through this wood full of cheer,
Remember to smile, for the fun's always near.
With each gust of wind, let your spirit take flight,
In this forest of laughter, all worries take flight.

Rhythms of the Natural World

The rhythm of leaves, they rustle and sway,
As chipmunks create their own cabaret.
With branches as drums, and berries as treats,
Nature hosts parties with funky heartbeats.

Caterpillars twist like they're in a grand show,
While fireflies flicker, putting on a glow.
And down by the brook, the tadpoles do jazz,
With frogs as the judges, giving thumbs up—how brazen!

The roots intertwine like a dance troupe so tight,
Making sure every critter feels cozy tonight.
Worms take the stage, in a silky parade,
While ants form a conga, swinging, unafraid.

So listen intently to the woodland's own song,
Where laughter and rhythm eternally throng.
In this symphony crafted by nature's own hand,
You'll groove with the rhythms that blissfully stand.

Secrets in the Shaded Grove

In a nook where the sunlight plays hide and seek,
The whispers of critters have secrets to speak.
The mice hold a council on crumbs they have found,
While the hedgehogs gossip about groundhogs around.

A badger in sunglasses surveys with a grin,
While ladybugs plot how to let the fun in.
And the trees twist their limbs, as if to share tales,
Of turtles in races and improbable fails.

Each shadow holds laughter, each rustle a cheer,
While the grasshoppers practice their stand-up routine here.
A fox tells a joke that sends everyone reeling,
In the magic-lit haven, where joy is revealing.

So wander this wonder, where giggles take flight,
In the corners of nature, where souls feel so light.
With secrets to share, and a smile for each day,
In this hidden delight, come frolic and play!

Dawn's Kiss on Dew-Kissed Petals

The sun peeks in with a playful grin,
Dewdrops dance like they're about to win.
A ladybug wearing a tiny crown,
Floats by a blossom, oh what a town!

A butterfly flutters, all colors abound,
Chasing its shadow, it tumbles around.
A grasshopper leaps with a cheerful croak,
While a snail rolls past in a lazy cloak.

A giggle erupts from beneath the leaves,
As squirrels play tag, tossing acorns like thieves.
The morning spills laughter, so bright and clear,
A waking woodland, come join the cheer!

In this merry dance of nature's delight,
The blooms all blush in the soft morning light.
With every whisper, the petals confess,
That waking up early can truly be a mess!

An Overture of Colors in the Thicket

The flowers debate which hue's the best,
Red claims the throne, while yellow's distressed.
Blue joins the fray with a bold little turn,
And orange just waits for its moment to burn.

A chubby bee buzzes, a judge from afar,
"Hey, stop the drama, you're all a bizarre!"
The petals just giggle, their colors unite,
Painting a canvas, oh what a sight!

Next comes a frog with a sly little leap,
"Just give me a chance, my kingdom I'll keep!"
But butterflies show him the true way to soar,
With grace and with flair, they create quite the roar.

In this colorful mix, a parade starts to form,
Nature's own festival, far from the norm.
Each color a story, each petal a dream,
Chasing away any thoughts that could deem!

The Stillness of the Enchanted Place

In shadows so deep, the mushrooms convene,
With hats oh so tall, they're quite the scene.
Whispers of secrets float through the air,
A squirrel starts nodding, says, "Life's not so rare!"

The rocks all chuckle, pretending they're wise,
With tiny sharp wits and the wildest of lies.
The ferns join the fun, swaying with glee,
As echoes of laughter spill out from a tree.

A breeze strolls through, with a skip and a hop,
"Did somebody say snack? I'm ready to stop!"
But the pixies are busy with glittery sprinkles,
Crafting the gigs that send everyone crinkles.

Here in this stillness, no worries to find,
Nature's own comedy, funny and kind.
The enchantment of peace wraps tight like a shroud,
And everywhere echoes, "Let's gather a crowd!"

An Ode to the Woodland Spirits

Oh spirits that dance in the twilight's gleam,
With sounds of the forest, you weave quite the dream.
A tickle of wind through your shimm'ring hair,
You giggle and twirl, without any care.

From nutty old trees, you concoct your brave plans,
Each squirrel your ally, each leaf in your fans.
"Let's throw a grand party!" you call out with flair,
And scatter your magic like sparkles in air.

The owls serve the snacks, their wisdom on point,
While raccoons act silly; they're right on the joint.
The moon winks above, a spotlight on cheer,
As you dance, spin, whirl, with no sign of fear.

Oh woodland charmers, with spirits so bright,
Forever you'll frolic in day and in night.
So let's raise a toast to the joy that you bring,
In this whimsical world, let us all dance and sing!

The Palette of Forgotten Tomorrows

In a world where socks go to hide,
Lost in the laundry, they're full of pride.
Painted in colors none can reclaim,
A swirl of chaos, yet it's all just a game.

When time takes a nap and dreams start to blend,
The brushes all giggle like they're best friends.
A canvas of chuckles, splatters of cheer,
Each hue tells a story, absurd but sincere.

But who needs a plan when you've got a cat?
It walks on the artwork, like that's where it's at.
With paw prints like sequins, it struts and it prances,
Leaving behind all the wild, funny chances.

So let's toss our brushes and dance with delight,
In a palette of laughter, we paint through the night.
For tomorrow will come, with its own silly tune,
But today let's just play beneath the bright moon.

Secrets Untold in the Canopy Above

The whispers of leaves, conspirators gleam,
They gossip of squirrels with wild little dreams.
A laugh from the branches, a tickle from air,
As birds share their secrets with flair and with care.

A raccoon in pajamas, he tiptoes with flair,
Claiming each acorn, he's quite the millionaire.
With a crown made of twigs, he'll rule like a king,
Defending his treasure while he dances and sings.

The sun filters down through a shroud of green veil,
While ants march in line, they'll never derail.
Each tiny little soldier has stories so grand,
Of crumbs they discovered across the vast land.

So listen real closely, the tales that they weave,
In the choir of nature, there's magic to believe.
For secrets, they linger, as shadows unfold,
In the canopy above, funny mysteries told.

Rays of Hope Beneath Twisting Roots

Under the twist of the roots, there's cheer,
Where worms throw a party, and they all disappear.
With hats made of mud, they dance underground,
Inviting the bugs to join in the sound.

The shadows are giggling, they bounce and they sway,
When light hits the surface, they hide away.
They peek from their hideouts to see what's the fuss,
As sunlight pours down with a warm, cheery thrust.

A funky old toad croaks a tune, oh so spry,
While puddles of laughter reflect in the sky.
Each ripple a chuckle, each droplet a grin,
As joy flows freely, like laughter within.

So celebrate each twist, embrace every turn,
Beneath the great roots, there's much to discern.
With rays of delight, let our spirits take flight,
In the depths of the earth, funny dreams take their height.

A Pilgrimage Through Sunlit Paths

On a quest through the sunshine, with sandals askew,
    I stumbled on laughter, and found quite a view.
With butterflies laughing, they twirled and they spun,
    In a dance of delight, under the warm sun.

There's chatter of daisies, sharing their news,
    With gossip of bees who have missed their queues.
    Each petal's a story, a chuckle, a tear,
    Gathering joy on this whimsical sphere.

The ants on their journey parade with such pride,
    Carrying crumbs that were meant to divide.
But as friends, they unite, with a gusto profound,
    For each little morsel brings fellowship 'round.

So onward I tread, with a hop and a skip,
    On this pilgrimage merry, a laugh on the trip.
For sunlit paths beckon with whimsy and cheer,
    In the heart of the moment, I find myself here.

Nature's Caress in a Shimmering Glade

A squirrel stole my sandwich, oh what a fuss,
He grinned at me cheekily, no need to discuss.
The sunbeams danced down, a spotlight so bright,
While birds in their choir sang tunes full of bite.

With butterflies fluttering, dressed up so neat,
They giggled while landing on my shoelace seat.
The flowers were gossiping, petals aflutter,
I laughed with a daisy, it called me a nutter.

Near a fountain so shiny, I tripped on a stone,
The frogs croaked in laughter; I wasn't alone.
A chipmunk waved wildly, his cheeks stuffed with snacks,
While I tended my pride, balancing on tracks.

The breeze blew quite gentle, a tickle of fun,
As I twirled and I stumbled, under the sun.
In this lively theater of nature's grace,
I danced with the ants, embraced the silly space.

Whispers Shared with the Wind

The wind whispered secrets, oh such a prank,
It ruffled my hair, like a mischievous tank.
Trees giggled and swayed, in a jesting ballet,
While I tried to hold on, what a goofy display.

Squirrels debated fruits, while perched on a branch,
One claimed a nut's size was quite worth a chance.
A butterfly swooped, donning a crown of fluff,
I chuckled and followed, feeling quite tough.

The clouds made a ruckus, racing in teams,
Challenging the sun with their fantastical dreams.
I watched as a thunderbird danced in the sky,
Practicing moves, oh my, what a flyby!

Each rustle and rumble was a playful tease,
Nature's own laughter floated on the breeze.
With echoes of giggles, sweet moments unfurled,
Joined in by the breeze, we spun 'round the world.

Footsteps on a Carpet of Leaves

Crunching leaves beneath me, a wonderful sound,
They laughed at my footfalls, twirling around.
The trees peeked and winked, green umbrellas of cheer,
I felt like a giant, from here to the deer.

A snail creeping slowly decided to race,
Yet he won with his patience, oh what a disgrace!
The rabbits were betting, with carrots on hand,
I joined in the fun, 'let's see who can stand!'

Each step was a giggle, a shuffle of grace,
A dance with the shadows, a whimsical chase.
My hat flew away, caught in a great gust,
Landed on a pumpkin; now that's a big bust!

The whispers of nature wrapped round my delight,
As I skipped over moss, feeling airy and light.
In the carpet of colors, this silly charade,
I'll waltz through the autumn, in laughter displayed.

The Breath of Existence in the Forest

In the heart of the woods, the critters convene,
H patch of mushrooms, a wobbly scene.
They chuckled and squeaked, sharing tales so grand,
While I scribbled some notes with a twig in my hand.

A turtle named Tim thought he ran like the wind,
But caught in a thistle, he humorously pinned.
A hare trotted by with a jaunty little flip,
Sneaking a snack as he made his escape trip.

The trees had opinions, barked out with pride,
"Let's toast to the sunshine!" they called, side by side.
Each whispering branch turned the laughter up loud,
As I joined in the merry, feeling quite proud.

Life here was a comedy, every leaf a new joke,
Sunbeams shared giggles; even shadows bespoke.
With nature's own banter, we spun tales so light,
In this playful existence, the world felt just right.

Raindrops and Reverence

In the chase of drops, we zoom,
Umbrellas twirl, making room.
Puddles splatter, boots make a splash,
Laughter erupts with every crash.

Fish might swim in shoes we wear,
While we dance with soggy hair.
Clouds chuckle, play hide and seek,
Nature's joke, oh how unique!

A snail's race, we cheer and shove,
Who knew wet could be this fun?
Bubbles bouncing with joyous glee,
Let's toast to puddles and glee!

With every drip, a giggle escapes,
Our two-left-feet make funny shapes.
Rainbows arch with a wink so bright,
In a splashy ballet, we take flight.

The Alchemy of Shadow and Light

Sunlight peeks, a cheeky glare,
Casting shadows without a care.
A cat on a wall, all stretched and snooze,
Effective camouflage while it snooze!

The tree seems to dance, despite no tune,
Waves of shadows, a silly cartoon.
Jump in the light, haunted by shade,
Hilarity strikes, all plans delayed.

Branches twist, giving poses a laugh,
Just don't ask the squirrels to do math!
In this theatre where shadows play,
We bring popcorn and laugh the day away.

A sunny wink, the light's a tease,
Wrapping shadows in quirky knees.
We wrap our smiles in this delight,
With the alchemy of shadow and light.

Solitude Wrapped in Foliage

Under leaves, I find my peace,
Nature's giggle never cease.
A squirrel chats, gives me a stare,
In this solitude, who needs a chair?

Branches whisper, secrets unfold,
Foliage hugs, a joy to behold.
Birds tell jokes, I raise an ear,
In my solitude, the world feels near.

A tiny ant with plans so grand,
Brings laughter as he grabs a strand.
Nature's chatter is quite the show,
Turning solitude into a flow.

Leaves pose as curtains, sure to please,
While the wind teases, begs for a breeze.
Wrapped in green, I chuckle with glee,
In this solitude, it's just me and tee!

A Journey Through Verdant Veils

Through green curtains, I skip along,
Nature's rhythm, a joyful song.
An owl hoots, a frog gives a croak,
Behind each leaf, another joke spoke.

A path of giggles, grass that trips,
Walking through foliage, toss the scripts!
Twirling leaves, I spin with delight,
As the sun tickles, making it bright.

Flora play hide and seek with the sun,
Petals dance, could this be fun?
A wiggle and laugh as I keep my grace,
A botanical floor show, my favorite place!

Through verdant veils, I trip, I twirl,
In nature's humor, lose my curl.
Every step, a chuckle bestowed,
On this whimsical, winding road.

www.ingramcontent.com/pod-product-compliance
Lightning Source LLC
Chambersburg PA
CBHW071828160426
43209CB00003B/234